T0268708

ALSO BY ISHION HUTCHINSON

FUGITIVE TILTS

FAR DISTRICT

HOUSE OF LORDS AND COMMONS

SCHOOL OF INSTRVCTIONS

FARRAR STRAUS GIROUX / NEW YORK

SCHOOL OF INSTR VCTIONS

A POEM

ISHION HVTCH INSON

Farrar, Straus and Giroux

120 Broadway, New York 10271

Map sketch of the terrain between Qasr al-Azraq and Hejaz Railway by

Lt. Col. T. E. Lawrence, 1918. Held by the National Archives, Kew.

Photograph on page 96 reproduced with permission of the Ministry of Defence.

The Library of Congress has cataloged the hardcover edition as follows:

Names: Hutchinson, Ishion, author.

Title: School of instructions : a poem / Ishion Hutchinson.

Description: First edition. | New York : Farrar, Straus and Giroux, 2023. |

Identifiers: LCCN 2023021272 | ISBN 9780374610265 (hardcover)

Subjects: LCGFT: Poetry.

Classification: LCC PR9265.9.H85 S36 2023 | DDC 811/.6—dc23/eng/20230508

LC record available at https://lccn.loc.gov/2023021272

Paperback ISBN: 978-0-374-61397-6

Our books may be purchased in bulk for promotional, educational, or

business use. Please contact your local bookseller or the Macmillan

Corporate and Premium Sales Department at 1-800-221-7945, extension

5442, or by email at MacmillanSpecialMarkets@macmillan.com.

www.fsgbooks.com

Follow us on social media at @fsgbooks

1 3 5 7 9 10 8 6 4 2

for Keith Burton
man in the hills

AND SOME THERE BE, WHICH HAVE NO MEMORIAL;
WHO ARE PERISHED, AS THOUGH THEY HAD NEVER
BEEN; AND ARE BECOME AS THOUGH THEY HAD NEVER
BEEN BORN; AND THEIR CHILDREN AFTER THEM.

—Ecclesiasticus 44:9

CONTENTS

SCHOOL OF INSTR VCTIONS

That rin-trah-la-la-la-
boom-wha-dis-boom-wha-dat-ra-ra-ra-
hottaclaps-inna-di-nitty-gritty-
rin-tin-tin-tin-I-Bop-I-own-the-trumpet.

Rin-trah-la-la-la.

Above deck, ice-scarred, off to Albion.

A boy struggles with a flag, crack-lashing
from his hands like a fer-de-lance.
Scorched, turning, watching.

Albion. Let it be named so. Furies
combed into heads, pressed into lines of boys
fidgeting with oceanic sorrows,
shouting "here, sir" and "not here, sir"
to ghosts on parade and at devotion,
leaping over shadows as the sea broke
with their names interred in the same roster.

Later they will climb the sea-charged cannons
and look up the school's purple and grey wall,
huddle in the breeze, quiet, awaiting
the bugle. Brass rasps the air iodine.
Then their scurrilous voices cross strict waves,
bound by an ardour to move while crouching
hidden in the open, an infantry
stalled in the holy metal of the sun.

Flecked dust and heat. Melting vellum. Lament.

The flag falls and

charcoal burners; shipwrights; tailors; clerks; fishermen;
motor engineers; blacksmiths; cooks; mechanics

whisks away in the grass.
Laughter sweeps across ranks. The chase earns him
his name: Godspeed. Godspeed! A khaki blitz
chorused their mute, fettered pain, the future's
fata morgana raging

sargasso eyes bulge as if a mirror lapses
time: Jesus of Lübeck? Braunfisch? No: iron twins
Karlsruhe and Dresden, incandescent drift amid
reefs at sunset rumoured to be wedding torches

to puncture
these poppies blackened with the unknown names
stung to their chests each morning like courtiers
of empire, primed to rake the playfield
where small wars erupted noon: "A Ras! A Ras!"
aimed at the Zion-haired boy, who mirrors
the sound, that broken water place gurgled
from poppies: the dread Arras.

Through wild
                    bells
he heard this, mouths gashed with ringing, fell in
ordered rows, tilted like ships in the glare.

This boy's passion for his *Britannica*,
its long-drawn leaves echo Vallombrosa,

off-key volumes buried now in his head,
or somewhere else, irrecoverably lost.

Will the flag rise like a kite's tail again
in air, like a headstone, accusing God?

Agog with corrosive dates in his book,
Godspeed shuttled between bush and school,
branching with delirium. He recalled
rain gauzed cannons with steam. Escutcheons
fluttered a red-letter day of sorrow:

> Every man who went from Jamaica to
> the front was a volunteer. 10,000.

Volunteer? *Bourrage de crâne.* Shadowed chains.
Sails, the air stagnate, white flashes of sharks
haunting fevers strangers shared in the hulls,
never to break after centuries on land;
perpetual flashes, perpetual sharks

trailing men who sang on the *Verdala*
in a blizzard to war.
                              Recover them.

They shovelled the long trenches day and night.

Frostbitten mud. Shellshock mud. Dungheap mud. Imperial mud.
Venereal mud. Malaria mud. Hun bait mud. Mating mud.
1655 mud: white flashes of sharks. Golgotha mud. Chilblain mud.
Caliban mud. Cannibal mud. Ha ha ha mud. Amnesia mud.
Drapetomania mud. Lice mud. Pyrexia mud. Exposure mud.
    Aphasia mud.
No-man's-land's-Everyman's mud. And the smoking flax mud.
Dysentery mud. Septic sore mud. Hogpen mud. Nephritis mud.
Constipated mud. Faith mud. Sandfly fever mud. Rat mud.
Sheol mud. Ir-ha-cheres mud. Ague mud. Asquith mud. Parade
    mud.
Scabies mud. Mumps mud. Memra mud. Pneumonia mud.
Mene mene tekel upharsin mud. Civil war mud.
And darkness and worms will be their dwelling place mud.
Yaws mud. Gog mud. Magog mud. God mud.
Canaan the unseen, as promised, saw mud.

They resurrected new counterkingdoms,
by the arbitrament of the sword mud.

So many,

    sugar; rum; cocoa; coffee; rice; logwood; bauxite;
    oranges, lime juice (for prevention of scurvy);
    mahogany propellers and 9 aeroplanes;
    11 ambulances; cotton (for balloons)

     15,600
drawn into the affray cousins make,
mortared to haul martyrs from mud trenches,
then the sand trenches, where the anonymous
sprung up a permanent humility.

    Recover,
ice-scarred, above deck,
              back to Old Britain.

Godspeed's wings clipped suspended air, then off.

—Quo vadis?

—Wha ra ra?

I

Now these were the embarkations they made to the HOLY
PLACES of EGYPT SINAI PALESTINE and of SYRIA in
the years of furies 1916–17 unto the last 1918. Godspeed
under the schoolyard's cherry tree scrawled his anabasis
marred by dust and the red smell of the RED SEA.

II

Disembarked for ALEXANDRIA shuck camp and enchained at MOASCAR and proceeded to EL FERDAN where it dechained and proceeded to REDUIT CAMP where it encamped and took over duties and post defenses in the sun.

He weighed the school's ungodly name: Happy Grove: an old cow pasture that once possessed the dispossessing Scottish Quaker founders. He weighed the name and found much wanting.

The strength of the battalion stood at 328 officers and 5321 other ranks.

III

It was around this time that he stood in the medicinal
green smell of his grandmother's room. Her brass bed
eroded of her glimmered with a hard spirit. DAMASCUS
in extremities. Slow-drawn agony at KUT. Trah-la-la-la.
Then proceeded to ABOUKIR for a course of instruction
at the R.F.C. through a gross waste of ammunition.

Regimental flags were hoisted. But Godspeed had crossed
flags from his mind and instead gazed sullenly towards
JERUSALEM.

IV

The founders left a splendid hoard of their bones in
  the cemetery gnawed into the trembling cliff. It was the
  land's only relic sunken in front of the chapel riddled
  phosphorescent with salt. March route to MEZERIB then
  through rough country without heather to encamp in
  the SHEPHELAH foothills west of JERUSALEM. At about
  4 miles inland Godspeed rode his devil horse top speed
  in the damp air of JIDDA to deliver his grandmother's
  cake order. Then moved by 2 barges to BALLAH for EL
  ARISH where many men sank beneath sand siloed in
  pharaonic doubt.

Brittle bible sheets of his Britannica ached countries
  under his thumbs. Uric acid steamed off skulls between
  UMBRELLA HILL and the tinfoil sea at SHEIKH
  HASSAN which was successfully assaulted and held by
  the battalion. He lifted his fingers there were new
  borders and some countries had changed their names.

V

His cousin Horace descended from JOB HILL and was taken in with cerasee tea and cream crackers and Chiffon margarine. Proceeded to ZEITOUN for courses of instruction in bayonet fighting. "Say the letters of the alphabet Horace" commanded Godspeed. Horace appeared to be palaeolithically stupid so Godspeed boxed him twice and said "Don't you know it isn't nice to fool Mother Nature?" as he walked out into the heat of the afternoon.

Then marched from GILBAN to DUEIDAR leaving "A" and "C" boys at HILL 70 and enchained for SUEZ to embark for BASRA to MESOPOTAMIA to join the dead already there.

VI

At Happy Grove Godspeed was instructed to penetrate
that sweet swan of AVON. Titters. But AVON. Where
was AVON? Must be over SHOTOVER or NONSUCH or
NORWICH or one of the easterly ridges of PORTLAND
galvanised with rusty shanties glinting off the bankrupt
Commonwealth sea.

36 horses were killed and 9 wounded and the remaining
123 stampeded off into the desert. The strength of the
battalion stood at 495 officers and 8953 other ranks.

VII

Some nights from his hole at BARRACKS LANE as the sugar
factory purred to sleep and the canes curled their tails
like fields of kittens he polished the moon to better
see Rosalie's face. Then proceeded to ROMANI in the
morning and moved to MAGDHABA by rail in the
afternoon. Two platoons formed escorts to prisoners
of war passing through the immemorial shade of the
staffroom. Their carbines shook flares out of the cherry
tree into his hair.

It was around this time a man named Pipecock Jackxon cut
off his ears at least that was what some boys mimed to
Godspeed in the chapel one devotion morning. The
broken fan was whirling like a lopsided angel. While
their heads were bowed for prayers Godspeed unclasped
his hands and threw a nub of magnet to the blade.
It stuck there uncertain as the destiny of the child.

VIII

And was shuck off the strength accordingly. ENGLAND.
    Heavy-clouded: that was the month of the death of
    the late Field Marshal the Right Honourable H. H. Earl
    Kitchener of Khartoum K.G. G.C.B. O.M. G.C.S.I.
    G.C.M.G. G.C.I.E. Colonel Commandant Royal Engineers
    Colonel Irish Guards Secretary of State for War that
    for a period of one week officers of the army shall wear
    mourning with their uniforms. On this melancholy
    occasion the boy wiped cherry juice on his lionized shirt
    in bad faith.

IX

Proceeded from MASADA to RHESAINA and then marched
through blizzard like young Herod and his mercenaries
marching to JERUSALEM under barrage of missiles in
the winter of 39–38 B.C. Then in a mighty dry day of
frost they proceeded to APAMEA where many dug
trenches with their bare hands. Two were admitted to
hospital for bronchial affections. It was like the *Verdala*
débâcle all over again. Godspeed coughed and his chest
was suddenly an exploding stone quarry. He wore the
wrong coloured shoes to school. Rin tin tin tin. Darkness
covered all of JUDAEA. He shook his jam jar of blinky
blink fireflies.

X

A great compost of The Gleaner and The Observer and The Star
grew by the pit latrine of his grandmother's house.
Having his weekend morning shit Godspeed objected
to the realist's prayer as he softened a page to tissue in
his hands which became marked with the black ink of
newsprint. Picric sand. Legions of flies flourished on
the dead and on the living.

He saw Taino arrowheads in the fashion of asters showered
out of the cherry tree and sizzled on the ground like
redcoats exterminated by myrmidon mosquitoes. He
winced at the name Bartolomé de las Casas which Horace
struggled to pronounce so Godspeed sprayed Baygon up
his cousin's nostrils and then proceeded to the Imperial
School of Instructions at MAMRE for a course in QF
13-pounder gun.

XI

Sobbing in the stairwell where he hid at lunchtime a sudden
  brunt of voices reached Godspeed. Prefects. Lickey lickey
  boom boom informer Sadducees. They prowled the
  hallways on behalf of the principal called Count Lasher
  behind his back because he neither spared the lash
  or the rod or the child and counted out the *sply-sply-sply*
  of his leather belt (soaked in kerosene oil) raising welts
  on backs and hands. The voices subsided in the waves.
  It was midday. The boy fell at ease.

Then proceeded to the trumpeting place and then swarmed
  to SEIR where they heard no call to prayers no hosannas
  but monoplanes and biplanes snorting overhead.

XII

Studying for the Caribbean Examinations Council (which he
loathed) Godspeed stayed up beyond midnight to watch
Sir Laurence Olivier as Hamlet. He dreamt thereafter
about school in WITTENBERG. And then proceeded to
PALESTINE and TYRE and SIDON where he caught a
glimpse of a wonderful dawn light which seemed to
refract mirages of ivory palaces that smelled of myrrh
and aloes and cassia. Men arrived from hissing
PASSCHENDAELE. Out blowing sinus. Windless sand.
A little right-hand mordent. *Quand les rats mangeront les
chats. Les Français prendront* ARRAS. Sand and glare.
Glare and sand. As his heart panted after Rosalie his
Shelamzion he wrote in his *Britannica* 'Long have I loved
thee O me puttus so ancient and new . . .'

4 officers and 32 men and 500 of the regiment's horses fell
to sunstroke in BIR BAYUD. Godspeed bookmarked an
entry in his *Britannica* with a beam of sunlight. Glare and
sand. Sand and glare.

XIII

An Inspector for Rural Schools visiting from KINGSTON
and sweating in a three-piece corduroy suit asked
Godspeed what his ambition was one morning after
devotion prayers. "Ambition sir?" "Yes." The word was
new to the boy. "To trample the enemies of the Lord sir"
the boy answered. The brilliantine hair visitor bristled
as Count Lasher drew near with his reeking
cat-o'-nine-tails unspooled.

Water lacked faith. He knew. Lack of water in the long
marches carved during the night between KULEH and
JERICHO was severe and faithless. His grandmother
sprinkled rosewater on his white shirt and khaki trouser
to iron them. The extreme heat and dust of the JORDAN
VALLEY could not be driven back and there in the place
of the first baptism many fell to polydipsia.

XIV

Godspeed stepped from a lenticular cloud and immediately
hid in the latrine stalls because the air whistled and
hummed with lickey lickey boom boom informers. He
stayed there until the sun gonged lunchtime when he
came out and hid under the stairwell and ate snapper
fried in coconut oil on white hard dough bread. He
peeled the skin off a shaddock and bit into the inflamed
heart as he listened to startled feet going up and down
the steps like the battalion scaling the small hills of
HARRAN. The earth trembled. The heavens dropped.
The clouds also dropped water. He felt refreshed.
Trah-la-la-la.

XV

Through the cemetery wearing his rubber tree leaf mask
   Godspeed sang: "Ya ho!" and again "Ya ho! Ya ho! Ya
   hoooo!" and "Long ago and long ago the pirates had their
   fun in the burning sun" and "Ya hoooo!" and "Sixteen
   men on a dead man's chest" and again "Ya ho! Ya ho! Ya
   ho!" and "A bottle of rum!" and again "Ya hoooo!" before
   disappearing in the mouth of the WADI SURAR wailing
   "A chi-chi bud oh!"

Hawk. Lark. Stork. Petchary. His command was over them
   all. He heard the dry exhalations of their wings as he
   fluttered across MOTHER FLOR'S BUSH to put down
   revolts in MECCA and MEDINA without once removing
   his mask.

XVI

Count Lasher's eyes bulged through every wall except
the Home Economics room. He overheard an inquisition
of the nunnery scene next door. Industrious belting for
suggesting that Ophelia was pregnant for Hamlet.

Iliadic swag. Rude boy quadrille. School after that summer
was a hospital ward for Godspeed who had fell on a blade
of cold steel on the playground. It stuck through his
tunic and left him with a green ache of gangrene. He
dreamt a bowl of guava. A blushing bowl of guava landed
on his chest when he woke. Splash.

The strength of the battalion stood a reed shaken penumbra
of God-fearers squinting with sand in their eyes.

XVII

Section drill and extended order drill and artillery drill
and artillery formation and attack formations and
the training of runners and observers and scouts and
musketry and embodying fire control and discipline and
description and recognition of targets and visual training
and judging distance and instructions in Lewis gun work
and bombing and rifle grenades and bayonet fighting
and rapid firing and intensive digging and hangar
construction: these were their School of Instructions for
the New Year.

XVIII

Dusk came to MA'ALEH LEVONA. The boy departed
mangling the words 'Dulce et decorum est' through the
Quaker cemetery. He climbed the steps of the chapel
ivied up to the bell tower of raw cinder and read
the school's motto *Ad agendum semper parati* painted in
purple on the wall: Always be prepared for piracy in this
drowsy lesser ELSINORE.

Obsolescent tanks. Slow moving pillboxes. Godspeed had
a severe bout of quartan fever delivered by Anopheles the
King's swanky messenger. It lasted several days and only
cooled when his uncle from the hills of AIRY CASTLE
took him there and anointed him with rum and left him
in a clearance bath of moon-soaked herbs. Ya ho.

The strength of the battalion stood at 29 officers and 974
other ranks. 7 died of exposure.

XIX

Dunce bats suffered interminable drowsiness their heads
drooping on desktops at the back of the classroom where
Godspeed sometimes sat doing his best to hide his
forbidden shoes under his desk from lickey lickey boom
boom prefects. It would be his last year at Happy Grove
when he topped the class and won nine Hardy Boys
novels and a tin case of The Oxford Set of Mathematical
Instruments Complete & Accurate by Helix. His mother
fainted with joy at the school's end-of-term prize-giving
ceremony.

Proceeded to RAFA which was bombed. He was thirsty so
he sucked the stigma of a hibiscus and later proceeded
through the half-wasted district stewed in the antiquity
of everyday cass cass and bangarang until he arrived at
BRYAN'S BAY beach where he last saw Banga his father.

XX

Cloudburst. The leap year was postponed when the
Governor General of JAMAICA Sir Howard Felix Hanlan
Cooke O.N. C.D. G.C.M.G. G.C.V.O. K.St.J sent carton
boxes of poppies to Happy Grove. Count Lasher and his
lickey lickey boom boom informers walked slowly down
rows in the chapel and placed a foreign petal in each
opened palm unknowing of what panic they had sown.

XXI

Cracked potholed macadam up to the groveless school.
  Heat waves strode in bronze. Horace forehead wrinkled
  terrified of grammar. During this period many
  officers and men were sent to the Imperial School of
  Instructions ZEITOUN for courses of machine gun and
  signalling and advanced telephone course and Lewis gun
  and bombing and strokes gun and general course of the
  compressed gold land. Horace asked Godspeed if John
  the Baptist could read. Godspeed answered by splitting
  Horace big taw marble into fissiparous chaff of glass.
  That day left between them a Milvian bridge never to be
  crossed.

It was around this time under circumstances short of no
  pomp and pageantry Godspeed's birth defect name of
  Ishi entered the school's roster so he unsettled the clear
  river in JABBOK and sank like a polished stone to its
  bottom.

XXII

They shovelled the long trenches day and night. Godspeed
remembered his aunt's velvet sadness through a keyhole.
She applied Pond's cream to her face in the mirror. Dun
voluptuousness. Her lover a cruise ship waiter lost
somewhere between PARADISE ISLAND and ATHOL
ISLAND. God was a wicked God to cripple so much
beauty.

What dreams flew behind the ragged eyes cut out of his
rubber tree leaf mask as he listened back for ya ho! Then
with a two-sided cutlass he cut down his father's trumpet
tree. The trunk rolled down into the abyss of the gully
in PEREA around the year 30 C.E. There Godspeed was
rocked with fresh cold. Coolie royal Rosalie retraced
herself to untouchable. And the battalion stood
thousands upon thousands of restless shadows casting
no shadows on the sand.

XXIII

Datura stramonium. Devil's trumpet. Godspeed found it in his
 Britannica just as some lickey lickey boom boom prefects
 circled around him under the cherry tree. They bound
 and brought him like Barabbas to Count Lasher who took
 him out to the cemetery and stood over him like an
 overseer (the cat-o'-nine-tails dozed on the principal's
 shoulder) and watched for hours as the boy wrote down
 the names of all the legible dead. Angel's trumpet.
 Jimsonweed the false Delilah of fealty and the alternate
 brain sweating between headstones.

Godspeed opened his ears not like the lid of a coffin but
 like the great stone rolled back from the door of the
 sepulchre to exhale gas and Christ.

XXIV

They moved from EL ANAB to LATRON under cover of
mist. His classroom was the first one by the opened
trenches and pit latrines. Leptospirosis spread rampantly
along the blocks of first and second form classes where
khaki boys go up and down the stairs through a
gas-cloud of flies. Bivouacked there for two years
Godspeed could not see the RED SEA. But he did see
Stone Haven the old great house shuddering in the heat
from the paroxysm of the forbidden Quaker romance
which took place there in the last century. It was that
tupping which ended the first missionary position of
SAINT THOMAS IN THE EAST. Et le temps passait vite très
vite.

XXV

And time was passing fast very fast as he stood still in
the medicinal green smell of his grandmother's room
with the conspiratorial cancers growing fast along her
spine. Godspeed knew the hell-ravaging pantomime
cannot be rehearsed and was there in CHALCEDON
when the West overcame the East and the silvered sea
below Happy Grove appeared to be one vast coffin.

Once on the way from school he collapsed into a sandpit
and his breath frayed into the hoarse final words of an
apostle. But Horace stretched out a hand and pulled
Godspeed from death. Then they journeyed up to BATH
FOUNTAIN where Horace sopped his cousin's chest
with the hot mineral water which a century ago healed
a runaway slave's wound.

The strength of the battalion stood at 37 officers and 1102
other ranks.

XXVI

Easterly to the sea. Waters of prophets at their feet after
trampling the fragile roads of reeds over CAESAREA.
They dipped and one was lost to save the life of a
comrade. When Godspeed waved a shy hand at Rosalie
from the road she darted through the thorn fence.
Sundown. Flecks of bright yellow flowers thrust up from
the mass of light baize foliage opened and then closed
behind her. Afterwards the body of 5640 Pte. G. C. Sealey
"D" boy found on the beach and was buried in a small
orchard south of the waters of prophets.

The battalion proceeded to LAKE TIBERIAS where no
enemy was seen or met with. All appeared quiet as it was
in CAPERNAUM after the host had passed and the end of
the world was played on the boy's cream plastic Yamaha
YRS-24B recorder.

XXVII

Out of a rising bank of fever grass he emerged wearing his
    rubber tree leaf mask. He pretended he was Baruch.
    "Weep not" he shouted. "Conquer and to conquering" he
    shouted. "Rejoice" he shouted. This was near or outside
    AXUM or ATLANTIS or those suicide goat cliffs near
    HECTORS RIVER where Horace leapt and became
    the Great Conjunction.

XXVIII

The moon was high up in RAMLEH. The surrounding
camps were bombed and machine gunned by enemy
aircraft that visited nightly. Bel the old back-of-bush
shanty shiftshaper blasting thunderbolts in RAMLEH.
Coolie royal Rosalie retraced herself to untouchable. The
southeastern sky was a single collapsing star. Rin tin tin
tin. He hid in latrine stalls from rickets-brained
Sadducees on patrol. Nocturnal birds cried out but only
one died because they were hidden in the moon
darkened olive grove of RAMLEH.

Then again at Christmas the boy's hands were high with
the murder of sorrel. He was told to whitewash the
long walls of Exodus Funeral Supplies & Services in
ANNOTTO BAY. Heat spangled the seaside as he
muttered in acute Estrangela: "Amen I was seized. Amen
again I was not seized. Amen I suffered. Amen again I
did not suffer."

XXIX

A polar moment of inertia. Lyddite and ammonal mud.
   On Heroes Day at Happy Grove the boy forgot the names
   of all seven national heroes of his island. He also moon
   mouthed the "Our Father" anthem: "Pest" for "bless"
   "slaughter" for "guidance" and dropped *booms* between
   JAMAICA: "JAMAICA" *boom* "JAMAICA" *boom* "JAMAICA"
   boom-sha-ka-la-ka: "land we love."

At the end of the month insane petrolic fever spiked
   the battalion which glowed like billions of archangels
   quivering with a fluorescent hum over honeycombed
   CANAAN. Quasar. Quasar. Dark matters all over again in
   the sun. The boy spat mouthful of sucked cherry bones
   into the sea then turned a fresh leaf of his *Britannica*.

XXX

In the Quaker chapel alone Godspeed stared at the white
angels and the luxe-hair Christ painted above the
baptismal pool. He thought of the nub of magnet like a
single black eye still whirling on the stalled fan. Then
proceeded through the reeds and hawks of UPPER
EGYPT to the tamarisks and hornets of LOWER EGYPT
and from there to JERUSALEM where No. 9265 Pte. J.
Floras "A" boy died from dysentery. *Ha-ha-ha-hassatan* he
sneezed and left the chapel. The stars went out and the
torches in the dark trembled like the curtains of
MIDIAN trembling to the wind.

Electric flares off the tips of horses' ears running forwards
with teeth clenched against the burning khamsin. The
battalion drifted in the distance and some of the very
foolish men swore they saw Hannibal crossing the ALPS.
Trah-la-la-la.

XXXI

Jamaica Broadcasting Corporation meteorologist Roy
Forrester promised rain. Once again no rain came. But a
hurricane the prime minister said was like HIROSHIMA
because it blew away all the island's fowls to FLORIDA
only to return as high tariff frozen chicken backs and
necks which Godspeed scorned and never ate. Then
proceeded with rapid succession to SHARTA and DEIR
SENEID 7 miles N. OF GAZA. Whilst there they saw
corpses and corpses of the dead from the 52nd Division
lying about. The men were repulsed by a charnel stench
they could not staunch. These were buried. Not in peace.

The battalion was equipped and issued box respirators PH
gas helmet being withdrawn and returned to ordnance.
The boy was issued a blue shell inhaler by visiting
Canadian nurses. He shook it and heard the babble of
End Times. A puff. Cloudburst in his shipwrecked chest.
He coughed and swore to bring about the Parousia.

The strength of the battalion stood at 24 officers and 915
other ranks.

XXXII

Rhythm please. From GETHSEMANE to SHASHAMENE
immanence repeat. Irredeemable Horace could be
Horatio as Godspeed was sometimes called Bop Pharez.
Rosa Rosa his arrhythmia. Piles of memorial stones
blooming off the foothills of MEJ DEL YABA resembled
uprooted zemis he once planted in his cove over at NAVY
ISLAND among roots and rocks and the secret names of
angels.

Then proceeded by enemy line to TELAIM. There they
remembered and sang: "Saul hath slain his thousands and
David his ten thousands." Bad boy anthem Godspeed
knew by heart since he last whistled in the bell-hushed
tower of Sunday School.

XXXIII

Rosalie retraced herself through the thorn fence.
 Mounted troops flanked on the DEAD SEA and the
 MEDITERRANEAN and then proceeded to BALLAH
 from DUEIDAR then to KANTARA and there by
 light-rail to GILBAN. Godspeed became a vulcanist. He
 brought his grandmother an enamel cup of boiled water
 and the room remembered.

Every day Haggadah. "Yea" said Godspeed winking one
 Jehovic eye at the sky adding: "is me that." Stiff
 opposition in ROMANI in late March and in SALHIA in
 late April and in the GREAT BITTER LAKE in early May.

Then the regiment formed to proceed into JERUSALEM to
 guard the HOLY PLACES as soon as they felt the slight
 tremours of God's feet on the land.

XXXIV

Quantus tremor est futurus! After a school visit to the Institute
of Jamaica in KINGSTON Godspeed heard the bell of the
drowned church of PORT ROYAL jangled in the nerves
of the island rusty with yellow fever. So went downhill
that BABYLON of hummingbirds hovering atoms of
emerald and amethyst and ruby washed with the casket
soda water of the CARIBBEAN SEA. *Quantus tremor est
futurus!*

And shuck off the strength accordingly. Godspeed mounted
his RUALLA horse and rode posthaste across the plain of
PHILISTIA to fetch water for his mother and drop off
cake orders for his grandmother. It was at this time a gift
of locks from the ladies of BARBADOS and a gift of
tobacco and cigarettes from the LEEWARD ISLANDS was
presented to the men of the battalion by the
commanding officer who did not understand why
the men of the battalion wept over such sour goods.

XXXV

The moon smote him by day. His face was a mist of water above his *Britannica* where he read "The island teemed with agoutis peccaries opossums racoons alligators iguanas and armadilloes" creatures evaporating off the pages and from the hills and gullies heavy with sunlight where he now set his eyes lunar and remote and full of years lightly borne with the breeze of history.

The first week of the new term Godspeed had asthma and was given a shot of unfiltered rum in molasses water and put to lay like a pasha in his grandmother's bed. On the third day a ghost brushed the blades of the basil and he looked through the backdoor at her sunlit wash heap. He could count even the invisible stones of the pile. His grandmother was there and wasn't there. He began to count and count the screes.

XXXVI

The sun smote him by night. He was writing a letter to his
   father in ENGLAND: "Dear . . ." the stars mirrored what
   he wrote but kept their distance. He shook his jam jar
   of fireflies blinky blinks and heard heavy cannonade
   blasting from the direction of HAREIRA. Bursting shells
   danced on the ridges behind ATAWINEH REDOUBT. He
   remembered that BELLAM was BETHLEHEM pitching
   between alms and lust. But he couldn't remember if Jesus
   was of NAZARETH or of BETHLEHEM or of GALILEE.
   A lateral skanking natty dread at the bus depot in
   GOLDEN GROVE told the boy that Jesus was of no
   place but here and touched his chest.

It was around this time No. 2292 Pte. Herbert Morris aged
   17 was executed for desertion by firing squad composed
   of 7 WEST INDIAN soldiers and 3 white soldiers. His
   soul fled to MIDIAN accordingly.

XXXVII

That night under the cover of dark Godspeed snuck out of
his grandmother's house to the Roof Nightclub. There he
saw earless Pipecock Jackxon spinning at the turntables.
Dub magnified his depression and his dread. The next
day at school sunlight fused to the leaves of the cherry
tree threw a stained-glass window at his feet. He kicked
against the pricks of the shadows and they shattered.

"Boy!" "Yes sir." "Who broke down the walls of JERICHO?"
"It was not me sir." "Stretch out your hand give me!" Even
before the cat-o'-nine-tails grazed his flesh the boy
started to bawl poppy-water.

XXXVIII

Running away from a lickey lickey boom boom informer
Godspeed looked back and screamed "Look for me in the
whirlwind!" and was then taken up into the air by a great
eagle. Ya ho.

XXXIX

Mud-caked men arrived from the DARDANELLES. They
kept their mouths shut while burying rabbit wires for
artillery at QUEENS HILL and didn't speak when they
ate their biscuits olives and dates spirited with sand.
Tanks well-spruced like white parasols sailed into the
oasis at KUT were surprise-bombed into new
illumination.

Godspeed fixed silhouettes upright one devotion morning
in the chapel. Their eyes were glazed from Count Lasher's
bullfrog sermon. Someone passed loud gas to the pitch of
the principal's voice a semantic *ignis fatuus* many asses
later paid the price for. Then proceeded from the DEAD
SEA to the slopes of MASADA where the battalion stood
at such and such and such officers and other ranks at the
end of the month Godspeed unplugged the sun and went
to bed.

XL

On moonless nights he saw through the pale leaves of the
coral caladium (his grandmother's potted hearts desire
lining a ledge of the veranda) praying they would sprout
into books by R. L. Stevenson and Archie Comics lit up
by his jam jar of blinky blink fireflies ticking between the
dishevelled pages quailing with the morning mist. Trah-
la-la. Pte. L. Killdeer "B" boy died from dysentery in
HEBRON. Godspeed also had a severe bout of
cogitationes malae which trembled his hands searching
through the thorn bush fence for Rosalie's fingers. Extra
karmic deposit the boy fell asleep in the merciless shade
of the schoolyard cherry tree.

It was at this time at the year's end 9191 Pte. J. A. Mitchell
was shot by order of field general court martial. His soul
fled to MIDIAN accordingly.

XLI

In his *Britannica* he found another BLUE MOUNTAINS
in Australia other than the ones behind his
grandmother's house. Filled with jealous rage he tore
out the entry page and stuffed it in Horace's mouth.
Blinky blinks strummed the dark back of his mind in
JUDAEA.

"B" boy proceeded from RAMLEH to YEBNA by march
route. Then the battalion proceeded to SHARKIYEH-
ES-GHARBIYEH by march route through fig trees and
apricot trees and almond trees. Surreptitious mosquitoes
by the billions. Anopheles bearing the King's messenger
bag on a branch from RAFA which was bombed to
SHELLAL which was not where Godspeed had a votary
of his own.

For dinner he ate EL DORADO's ackee and shat in the
piratical patch of pure blue water across from his house.

XLII

And ALBION the sugar factory in RAMLEH and its
surrounding orchards were blanketed by the same locusts
that blemished the RED SEA in 1446 B.C. Some said
creole bread with margarine was the black man's manna.
Or potato pudding which had hell on top and purgatory
at the bottom and heaven in the middle.

Manna was real if somewhat jaundiced. Then a Lada
backfired history on the Quaker hill and out stepped
Devastation in high heels. Signal fires were burning at
LACHISH. Pte. James Davidson "C" boy was beheaded in
MACHAERUS bespattering the sand with little blood.

XLIII

It was wash day. Godspeed went to the public standpipe and
brought back a large bucket of water for his grandmother
who stood hunched over her unspeckled ARARAT laden
with his khaki and white shirts. Rosalie was as black as
him yet invisible when he saw her at the thorn fence. He
waved to her. She vanished.

High winds blew the sea stone blind and then hail and sleet
fell throughout the month when Godspeed up at STONY
HILL put down his bucket and it clattered in the day
of the great slaughter when the towers fell and water
dripped like blood in the boy's eyes.

XLIV

No. 1391 Pte. J. Fisher "C" boy died pneumonia.
Bismillahirrahmanirrahim.

The battalion less "B" boy enchained for EL ARISH.
Bismillahirrahmanirrahim.

No. 134 Pte. A. M. Harper "D" boy died pneumonia.
Bismillahirrahmanirrahim.

"A" boy proceeded to No. 3 School of Military Aeronautics
for course in aviation. Bismillahirrahmanirrahim.

No. 6898 Pte. Benn "C" boy died malaria.
Bismillahirrahmanirrahim.

Bismillahirrahmanirrahim. Bismillahirrahmanirrahim.
Bismillahirrahmanirrahim.

XLV

Wild butchery of souls blossomed in the desert.

It was pitch-dark night in JANE ASH CORNER when
   Godspeed shook his jam jar of fireflies. Blinky blinks
   bursting occasional sparks like fireworks going off faint
   and distant N. OF GAZA.

No rest for Rosalie. Rosalie. Rosalie. Ever rushing to the
   biting calls of her name from the ash yard. And this was
   the month the body of No. 221 Pte. W. Smart "A" boy
   was brought in by a party of SINAI police. Camp was
   surrounded by 221 sandgrouses that could not be chased
   away.

XLVI

He braided his many dreadlocks into one thick Horus lock
and implemented a fixed fee to read the newspaper on a
plaza in JANE ASH CORNER SQUARE. "I am troubled
with my head and cannot stand the sound of the guns"
No. 2776 Pte. Winston Thomas of CLARENDON told the
courts: "I reported to the doctor and he gave me no
medicine or anything sir. Everything hurts me sir."

Summon these things for healing: his grandmother's torn
scarf self-hymned with camphor and basil fading
through fading saffron. Her dress intact on the
clothesline awaits the shape of the breeze from AMITY
HALL.

It was still pitch-dark night when Godspeed shook his jam
jar of fireflies and blinky blinks illuminated the
woodworm boards and desolate GOLGOTHA.

XLVII

ENGLAND: called to be God's saved and saving nation
   overran with messianic claimants since before
   the crusades. At Easter Godspeed ate spiced bun and
   bilirubin cheese of Christ's flesh and tissue and drank
   rum-spiked eggnog of the Lord's blood. Euangelion.

Then marched to IPSAMBUL to see the Garden of Eden in
   the cave there. Back at Happy Grove Godspeed inverted
   Zion into noise. He also turned zero backwards to reveal
   the true distance between MOUNT MEGIDDO and
   MOUNT ZION for which Count Lasher raked the beaded
   cat-o'-nine-tails over the boy's palms.

XLVIII

The hills at SOLLUM were covered with thousands of white
figures. Angels? Ghosts of fathers? Exhaust fumes from
the sugar factory receded like waves in the dark. Then
the whole of the plains of JUDAEA shuddered into a
mixture of sand and mud and water as he stripped to his
torn underwear and washed himself on the surface of
the concrete lunate cesspool beneath the stars of his
grandmother's house.

Morning turned noon under the flowering Indian maple
during Social Studies class. There he fastened a crown of
hibiscus on his head and struck pharaoh ants from his
shins. They twinkled in the dust blinding the WAY OF
HORUS.

XLIX

Then proceeded to BAGHDAD and AMMAN. Godspeed was
almost afraid of butterflies. They sickened him during
the breeding season when they swarmed around any
source of water in the viceregal district where he was
born. The day was hot and everything was green. He saw
that the puddles were moving and the cars were crushing
butterflies and the roads were moving too because the
butterflies were slowly dying on the roads. Everything
moved around him. The leaves on the trees swayed not
from the wind but from butterflies. Butterflies were
everywhere alive on the blooming lilacs and dead on the
roads. He ordered a hurricane to wipe the roads clean
and immediately Bogle danced into the shutting fan of a
shame-me-lady.

Crossed country without a scarp of cover through the
wildflowers of WADI BALLUT the men proceeded to
TAHPANHES where weeping was ceaseless.

L

This time two weeks before his 13th birthday the Antichrist
Pope John Paul II visited his island. With a stub of coal
Godspeed drafted new statutes for the Court of Star
Chamber on the plyboard side of the school's latrine. He
stepped back to admire his new minted theology. "These
are no competent judges of the doctrine of God in Christ
but must be overthrown" it declared. It also declared:
"Vatican don't instruct I I instruct Vatican."

The strength of the battalion stood at 603 officers and 7130
other ranks.

LI

The battalion proceeded to MILLO to fortify the old city
walls. In the middle of a marl road snaking between
tall canes Godspeed met Pipecock Jackxon wearing a
necklace of two flattened Coca-Cola corks sweat stuck
to his chest. Urim and Thummim he called them. Seven
John crows flagged out of SOKHO when he strung the
corks around the boy's neck.

Then to the clashing silver green sound of the canes he said:
"I Pipecock Jackxon Jack Lightning Jesse the Hammer
Lee Scratch Perry Daniel Dandelion the Lion I am the
flying fish. I boom Death and I boom debts and I bust
bets and I win bets and I sin Death and I kill Death with
my fate lock. Behold! I conquer Hell with my Merry
Christmas bells. I am a walking talking time boom.
Dandelion the King of ZION."

LII

Maybe Godspeed was a beastly sort of Baptist Caliban who
knew that bishops and deacons and pastors and priests
were all waterless canals and nothing but heretics
schismatics and hypocrites of the Ixodidae order cut by
dry watercourses he watered with his wee-wee from his
chamber in LEBANON. Scrape trencher 'Ban 'Ban
Cacaliban!

Proceeded to GIBEAH where No. 1996 Pte. O. Harris who
carried sassafras twigs mint leaves foxglove flowers and
sheaves of tobacco in a sachet in his pocket detonated
into thousands and thousands of moths. And the curtains
of MIDIAN did tremble.

LIII

Embers under the yabba. 6322 Pte. I. McKenzie "C" boy died pneumonia.

Sparks to the corn sheaves. Proceeded to SUEZ for embarkation to MESOPOTAMIA for rations of radishes onions and garlic bulbs. No. 921 Etc. App. C. H. "B" boy killed accidentally by grenade.

Clapping flies off his grandmother's bakes Godspeed pronounced "I am Lord of the Houseflies" so loud all the dogs on STONY HILL began to bark just as Horace limboed below the line of the horizon which simply meant that Horus the Christ has risen.

Thyme rosemary sativa. Luminescent smoke. He pinned a gashed poppy to his uniform shirt and it bled anew. Obed's seal.

LIV

Also on the marl road which was between PEACOCK HILL
and HOLLAND BAY Pipecock Jackxon gave Godspeed a
parchment scroll scribbled over with Xs in blue and red
felt-pen ink. The boy rubbed the two beaten Coca-Cola
corks together and ignited twilight.

LV

Godspeed skulled elocution day at Happy Grove and so
missed the shrieking out of "And then my heart with
pleasure fills, / And dances with the daffodils." Bayonet
fighting amid the cactus hedges the metal tangled with
the sand's imperfect memory in the wood of EPHRAIM.
He sprinkled spikenard on his head and replenished his
jam jar of fireflies as if they were gold coins of fluctuating
bullions in the deep dark of night.

He was called to whitewash the walls of Prestige Funeral
Supplies & Service by the seaside in PORT ANTONIO
where his grandmother's body was laid out for the final
burial rites. He decreed a calendrical change and her
laminated almanac saviour was taken off the kitchen
wall. He heard the far-off drum of Miriam as he paced
with a sharp ringing in his ears among his grandmother's
croton plants which glittered like sardius like topaz like
diamond like beryl like onyx like jasper like sapphire
like emerald like carbuncle like gold like a green ringing
green of mildewed croton leaves he would if could
scatter on the turquoise sea.

LVI

Dead night. He climbed into the foothills of the BLUE
MOUNTAINS to see the sons of Obadiah chanting down
stars. They shook sparks out of their lion manes flashing
in the bonfire dark where Pipecock Jackxon hovered
licking Xs with the flame onto his scroll. Detachment at
BOZRAH for MAZAR ABD and ROMANI there 9011 Pte.
A. Taylor "C" boy died from pneumonia. His soul flew to
MIDIAN accordingly.

Godspeed was summoned to the gates of LIÈGE to
watch Pte. 8308 Colin Morgan expelled for kissing or
doing something worse to Prudence O'Hara at the back
of the chapel. The Quaker ghosts roused their heads from
the graves and their bones ticked te te le stai on repeat.

LVII

Foxes cobras sand snakes locusts eagles vultures desert
hares desert mice scarab beetles and men levitated in
the mirage on the march to BASRA. Under 'comment' on
the boy's final report card at Happy Grove Count Lasher
wrote 'lacks aptitude and out of order.' Godspeed tore up
the card and scattered the pieces in the orange quailing
heat of the frangipani and then pressed his rubber tree
mask between pages of his *Britannica*. The mask will
dry to a tobacco brown. All in this bitch of an epoch.
Confound the bitch.

"C" boy platoon proceeded to guard over war matériel
captured at HUJ and SIMSIN and NEJED and TUMRAH.
Then the battalion less "B" boy proceeded to ESDUD by
march route across country where the transport had to
be abandoned in the sand where they resembled melting
spiritual icehouses.

LVIII

Count Lasher died of fatal stoppage of water. That was a lie.
The principal didn't die but had a rum stag week in NEW
KINGSTON where he was found in the back room of
Caesars Exotic Night Club his rum eyes reddened by
chronic conjunctivitis hiccupping to the women of their
archaic profession of balm and disquiet: "Hedication is
hall in hall me hambition . . ." "Wha ra ra him say?" said
one to another in the strobe-lit mirror. Trah-la-la.

The strength of the battalion stood at 67 officers and 7408
other ranks of hebdomads which proceeded to encamp
in SAMARRA then in DEIR EL-BAHARI where the men
decanted pretend beer out of latrine buckets into their
mess tins and made small gods out of themselves in the
desert though their minds made of sand still grew
conscious and sad.

LIX

Moonlit rainbow on Christmas Eve. The NILE was violet
and the MOKATTAM HILLS were rosy in colour. Micro-
cocci ate away flesh down to the bones and further down
to the soul. The strength of the battalion stood at 645
officers and 1700 other men proceeded to EMMAUS
across the painful clearness of the sand infinite as the sea.
One held a sprig of psalm against the frosted distance.

Then they withdrew through barrage of fire along WADI
SIHAN to WELL FARM and proceeded to ATAWINEH
along GAZA-SHERIA ROAD where large clouds of
dust resembling the elephants of Antiochus were seen
threshing in mortal pain in the direction of HAREIRA.
Godspeed's mind pierced into the imperial pachyderm
and issued a Raphia Decree out of the pillars of the limbs
of the cherry tree. *Vespasian Vespasian Vespasian* fritted the
leaves. Hasten slowly.

LX

The ridge EDOM poto poto with sunset. There Godspeed's
friend to be rung with tyres and burned alive lived. To
get to EDOM they passed through CAINA and LOVE
LANE. He saw Sirius burning above the acacia trees of
LOVE LANE. Grinding out counter-blazon on a crisp
page of his exercise book Godspeed hierarchized the
afterlife lifting his friend above Saint Dismas. Rosalie.
Rosalie. Rosalie. He shook his jam jar of fireflies blinky
blinks and whispered "I am going to show you my
motion I am going to jump in the ocean."

Dub drunk Godspeed stumbled out of the Roof Nightclub.
He walked through the town strung with doused pepper
lights to the harbour following the foetid predawn
December scent of the swamp. Out of NAVY ISLAND
crust of scarlet ibises rose with the sun and magnified
the cherry-magnified boy who felt keenly fractures in his
bones clicking like wings. "The pirates had their fun in
the burning sun . . ."

LXI

The furies of ALBION raging their subterranean secrets
   entered the true Kingdom of HAM while Godspeed
   swindled from a Canadian missionary a pocketsize blue
   Gideon bible with the golden amphora smudged to a
   light brown stain. Ya ho. Pestilence of switchblades not
   locusts rode on the wind across SINAI and in GOSHEN.

No. 46 Sgt. A. V. Chan "A" boy killed in action on the
   ROMAN ROAD between GRANT RIDGE and
   BAGHALLAT. He was buried at the foot of
   MUSSELABEH. *Veni redemptor gentium* sang the celestial
   voice men of SAINT VINCENT. Yes come gently. Gently
   like the small rain of rosewater murmuring from a black
   hand.

LXII

It was around this time Count Lasher cut off Godspeed's
dreadlocks. His mother slapped the daylights out of
the principal and was thrown into the jail at GOLDEN
GROVE. There was a blackout. The constable's badge
brightened up the sky over SODOM. Godspeed wept in
his khaki as by GAZA when Samson felt the pillars
convulse in his palms and wept.

Rosalie laughed a trembling hibiscus laugh in the thorn
fence. Godspeed held it in his throat until it stung even
in his dreams. Or maybe her laugh was a dream petalled
in his head when he saw her vanished for good into
that ash yard. Rosa hibiscus Rosa hibiscus Rosa hi . . .
exploded in RAFA which was bombed into baffled
prayers. Ha ha ha mud.

At the beginning of the month the battalion was a flurry of
unstirring flags on the horizon line.

LXIII

He lit tails of foxes mongooses cats snakes and cousins with
lightning. He poured rubbing alcohol in his jam jar of
fireflies and set the blinky blinks ablaze. He was knife
scissors razors with a sharp ringing in his ears and bald
head and he hid in the bosom of stars bald and chalked a
circle of misery bald to place every principal in and then
buried the sheaves of his head bald and with a jackass
jawbone he stormed the jail and fed his mother roasted
corn thundering "It is easy to remember and hard to
forget I Bop I own the trumpet I am the Gorgon."

To fierce Kumina drumming and rum at midnight No. 46
Sgt. A. V. Chan soul flew to MIDIAN accordingly.

LXIV

Then into MOUNT EPHRAIM and SHARON then on to
JERICHO and AMMAN then through SAMARIA to
GILEAD and GALILEE then on to DAMASCUS and
finally through the gross darkness of CANAAN to
SHILOH the battalion glimmered its nocturnal corolla
of petals towards its last School of Instructions fragrant
of memories chastened of sacrifice sweetened of
resignation quickened of hope in the front line for
untold harm to carry ammunition to do the general
work or something like that to simply be men merciful
men whose righteousness must not be forgotten.

After Godspeed lost the precept of his head he lost his mind
and found it in the larvae of bees outside EIN GEDI
where he exalted himself like a young palm tree. He wept
again this time into song for he knew where there was
anger there will be grief.

LXV

The following other ranks boarded at "M" Special Hospital
at ABBASSIA awaiting passage to the WEST INDIES. Dark
matters in the sun they resembled prehistoric hills of
charcoal soaked by rain mouthing bits of the Sixth Book
of the Maccabees. In KANTARA one handed his lice eaten
mantle to the other and neither saw death nor his island
home again then proceeded by barge to TARANTO.

LXVI

That night by his jam jar of resparked blinky blinks fireflies
and to his grandmother's wheezing and with the Urim
and Thummim and his *Britannica* he deciphered the Xs
on Pipecock Jackxon's parchment scroll:

"The moon the stars the sun the clouds the world the globe
the universe the equator the galaxy everything is in my
eye. I kiss the Earth and thunder roll. This is the truth
and nothing but the truth so help me true and living
God. 144,000 Mosquito Angels sting with lightning
pssssst! 'Enjoy death' say the dead birds and 'Enjoy death'
say the dead animals. Ha ha ha! We laugh."

The boy made a mitre of the scroll to guide his oncoming
dreams.

And some there be which have no memorial
And some there be which have no memorial
And some there be which have no memorial
who are perished as though they had never been

and are become as though they had never been born
and are become as though they had never been born
and are become as though they had never been born
and their children after them

LXVII

The strength of the battalion stood at 32 officers and 871 other ranks at the beginning of the month and 23 officers and 767 other ranks at the end of the month of four hundred years of affliction.

Noon. Thursday 31st October 1918 it all ceased. That night Godspeed slept and wandered the tormented olive groves of TARANTO. Achan's ghost stalked the boy. And the curtains of MIDIAN did tremble when he woke and murmured a memorial for Pte. A. Denny who at that time was shot by a firing squad. Melting vellum.

The strength of the battalion at the beginning of the month stood at 23 officers and 786 other ranks and at the end of the month 31 officers and 1171 other ranks. Not in peace but appeasement they were disembarked to their islands. They were not met with harps and timbrels but the blue ice of COCYTUS quiet as the CARIBBEAN SEA. That rin-trah-la-la-la. Selah.

ν

Dark roughened by flares could be cane fire
machete men entered and returned, charred
as overseas they withstood similar
spectral absence, reduced to shell-humpers,
quiet volcanic plugs left to caustic
vigils amid flaks of tares. Some survived.
Black luminosity. Some survived.
(They went on, back with wounds which never healed.)
Still, others did seep into the landscape,
neither degraded nor with dignity.
Dark matter, all over again, in the sun.

Who mattered was what mattered. What mattered
more than the irrecoverable loss
was the gain. Mammon greased every slime pit.
From excreta, gold; entrails, oil; blood, bonds.
Whatsoever might be spent, whatever
could not redeem, was brutally tendered,
like auctions circled by loan sharks at ports.
(Perpetual sharks.) In parenthesis,
the finical chase lured through history,
which, 'To Whom It May Concern,' concerned naught,
mattered insofar as change itself was
tacit wealth: maggots turned magnates; kites kine
slaughtered in coffers. Offal shrunken black
as burnt florins' heads. Cephalophore.
Savings then, as now, meant another grace,
for which they suffered the ultimate wage.

Where the sun never conceded to light,
now lit. Even still, belated justice
does not reflect where it must show: England:
leave room for the beloved below;
recover them all, for belated praise.
A whiff of incriminating cherries
holds beneath the meridian blue,
raises choppy flatlines of the Atlantic
into vertical columns, heavenwards,
which is the earth. Earth which is their bodies
that have crossed, above deck, the sea-earth,
and give the earth a lasting heritage,
and the sea the broad church of night and day.

Source of echo
madman of prophecies
buffering nonsense
in absence of anything
solid as cloud
flung
from the womb
pale pallid asteroid
belt of nanny goat

conjuror of the ill-spoken
adlibbing in shadow
a race in a curve
as an old woman's palm
billows the blue light
instance of an ant's
legs twitch beneath
the headless Nobody
trickster and soothsayer

burner of Ark
cutter of dub
double-talk lame-walker
translating ship screams
and the long gazes
and the neck cricks
and the hollow face

celestial and earthbound
posing the first question
to God after an eagle
picked your liver
and tell the reply
in the treetops
to hold still

and accept
fade and descent
into nothing
like a scribbler train
heading into a bright
blind and flat
as the mouth hole
of some strange being
and what you say
at the controls
picking up signals
and feedback
off the metallic horizon
and the purple field

where a girl
undoes her hair
and warps herself
around a tree

her mother is buried
under the grass
there you once wept
from whence comes
something longer
than a shadow
when a shadow
falls in the desert

and the hills expire
the sea expires too
for you outlived
your mule days
of packed crocus
and blades of sun
ripe on your back
at the river
like a crab catcher
in shortcuts
rancid with obeah
on your skin
for a few shillings
to blast off downtown

praise your tongue
praise your spirit
praise your madness

in praise of fern
in praise of shame-me-lady
in praise of bushel
in praise of hanging leaves
in praise of praising

your word mass
your mix match
your jamming of elements

when things get terrible
and times get dread
you're ahead

praise
praise
praise

у

TO THE MEMORY OF THOSE WEST INDIAN SOLDIERS
WHO FOUGHT IN BRITISH REGIMENTS DURING
WORLD WAR I ESPECIALLY THOSE WHO PERISHED IN
THE MUD AND SAND OF THE DESERT DURING THE
MIDDLE EASTERN CAMPAIGNS OF 1916–1918 AND TO
THE VETERANS WHO RETURNED TO THEIR ISLANDS
TO CARRY ON THE GREAT WORK OF INDEPENDENCE
FROM THAT COUNTRY WHICH HAD FIRST SENT
THEM TO THEIR PAIN AND DEATH THIS POEM IS
ENGRAVED ESPECIALLY TO THE MEMORY OF THOSE
SONS OF PORTLAND IN EASTERN JAMAICA WHERE
THEIR NAMES ARE HERE ETCHED NOT BY DIVESTITURE
BUT BY INVESTITURE TO THE LAND AND SEA WHERE
THEY WERE BORN AND THEIR BLOOD STILL ECHOES
E. M. ABENDANA S. WILLIAMS L. MOORE J. DOUGLAS
A. C. SMITH J. ANDERSON S. MING E. ALLEN
L. A. MURRAY G. BROWN H. WILSON L. FOWLES
P. BROWN F. L. A. DUNN I. GISCOMBE W. DEACON
C. SMITH L. A. DUFFUS E. ANDERSON H. FINN
W. FRASER J. PHILLIPS W. M. GOFFE A. BROWN
I. ANDERSON E. MAINE T. ANDERSON J. MYRIE
N. ALLEN T. WILLIAMS D. DACUS T. B. KEECH
J. MITCHELL R. OAKLEY J. NICHOLS H. PHILLIPS
J. BURRELL R. ROBERTS W. MOORE R. SHERWOOD
H. BURKE C. SKYERS J. T. WILLIAMS A. WEBBER
W. WILLIAMS A. MODDIE E. ASHLEY J. WALKER. E. DYCE

ACKNOWLEDGEMENTS

Grateful acknowledgement is made to the Academy of American Poets Poem-a-Day, *The American Scholar*, *The Atlantic*, *Columbia Journal*, *Liberties*, *The Paris Review*, *Ploughshares*, *Poetry*, *The Poetry Review*, *Provincetown Arts*, *Raritan*, *The Yale Review*, and *The New York Review of Books* for publishing parts of *School of Instructions*.

I am indebted to the kind support of 14–18 NOW, BBC Contains Strong Language, the British Council, the Joseph Brodsky Rome Prize, and the Civitella Ranieri Fellowship. Special thanks to the Imperial War Museums in London.

School of Instructions was co-commissioned by Karen McCarthy Woolf for the centenary of the First World War. An earlier version appeared in *Unwritten: Caribbean Poems After the First World War.*